Think like a Real Estate Investor

Darrell

Great to know
you

THINK

like a Real Estate
INVESTOR

MARC PELLETZ

CONTENTS

ACKNOWLEDGMENTS

This book would not have been possible without the countless mentors who have guided me throughout my life. I want to say thank you to them and to all the experiences I have had until now, whether or not I enjoyed them at the time.

A very special thanks to my wife, who put up with my 3 a.m. mornings during the creation process.

A big shout out to Pete Adams. Without his help this book would not have been completed on schedule.

To Anne Pyburn Craig for her editorial eye, and to Audria Wooster of Indigo Design for putting it all together beautifully.

Last but not least, I am grateful for the intelligence source I call God that made all of this possible.

Marc Pelletz

FOREWORD

This little book shares what I have learned from over 40 years experience in real estate, studying with some of the great mentors and accumulating personal experience. It's inspired by creative intelligence.

It's not a how-to manual, but a starting point on the road to becoming all you can be. Only you can draw the road map. This book is intended to stimulate a sense of possibility and get you to take that first step toward realizing all of your dreams.

The concept that "thoughts are things," that we co-create our own reality, has been understood for centuries. When you apply the concepts in this book, you are tapping into a scientific system that will transform your life.

Readers of self-help and personal development literature will immediately understand that I am not the original source of the ideas in this book. They have been presented many times over the centuries, in many different forms.

The words I have chosen to express them are my own best expression of the ideas I live by, sourced from the Universal Creative Intelligence. Any resemblance between my phrasing and that of the excellent authors listed here, or that of anyone else, is accidental.

Chapter 1

DESIRE

"The starting point of all achievement is desire."

- Napoleon Hill

All great successes in life come from our thoughts. Before we achieve, we must first conceive. But our thoughts must be infused with a burning desire.

Having that burning desire is essential to continued movement in the direction of what we want.

I have found this to be true in anything I have wanted to accomplish. Along the journey of greatness there will always be obstacles and challenges. To push through them, you must cultivate a burning desire and let nothing get in its way. It's your rocket fuel.

Any achiever understands that a burning desire comes before any great achievement. You have to want it so bad you can taste it.

A burning desire creates a state of mind that will generate the energy and vibrations to attract all that you need to accomplish what you want. A burning desire drives action.

A burning desire permeates and penetrates every cell of your being. It clarifies your thinking and motivates exactly what you need to do to achieve your goals.

This is not to say other parts of your life are unimportant. But to achieve your dreams, you must have a set of priorities that direct each day's activities. Making progress toward life goals will energize every part of your life.

When you have a burning desire and can work your mind and energy into a goal-oriented frenzy, you'll begin to notice how life will fall into place. Fortunate "coincidences" will begin to unfold as you apply the universal laws of energy.

When I was a young man, just over 21, I made the decision to begin my real estate career. I remember how passionate I was and my willingness to do anything I could to have the freedom I envisioned as my future. I read books, watched infomercials, studied people who had what I wanted to attain, and made a decision to do whatever it takes. I had a burning desire.

What I didn't have was money. I actually called my parents to see if they'd help me buy that first house, and they said no. Being a defiant child, this made me all the more determined! Another path opened up before me. It wasn't long before I had my first success.

It was a burning desire that got me that first house. Without a burning desire, I might have accepted that "no" and settled for less in life.

I took my desire and ran with it, and before I was 25 years old I had accumulated over 100 rental properties in Phoenix, Arizona.

I wish I could say that it just got better from there. But life wasn't done teaching me. (It never really is, if you pay attention.) There were lessons I needed to learn to get to where I am today.

At 41 years old, I had to start all over again, and a burning desire isn't just for the young! I was able to tap back into the creative force, get that burning desire fired up again. This time, I had more than just a burning desire. I took what I'd learned from success and from disaster and implemented the strategies that I will share in the remaining chapters of this book.

Chapter 2

DECISION

"Nothing happens until you decide. Make a decision and watch your life move forward."

- Oprah Winfrey

Making a decision is a powerful act. It directs your burning desire toward a plan of action.

I sit here in Breckenridge writing this book that I've wanted to write for at least two decades, and since you're reading it, it's now a reality. My burning desire to write it was finally strong enough to overcome that inertia. So I made a decision: it would be finished by the end of January. I made a plan of action, and the universe — the energy web, if you will — has led me to the right places and the right people at the right moments.

Without a decision, your burning desire is useless. Many people desire to do many things — quit smoking, lose weight, master a new skill — but fail to make the firm, unshakeable decision that makes it happen.

A committed decision is the key to defined, purposeful action.

If your burning desire and commitment is to make real estate your path to financial freedom, you must determine what area of real estate you want to pursue. There are incredible opportunities in this field, but only deciding which area you want to specialize in can help you determine exactly what action to take. Whatever you may choose, a burning desire and a committed decision are your fuel and your North Star.

At 41 years old, basically broke, I found my burning desire still alight inside me. I made a committed decision to get back into real estate, and set a goal of having 50 rentals by the time I was 50. I wrote it on a 3 x 5 card and imprinted that image on my brain every day. I visualized what it would mean to me, felt the feelings that would come with success.

THINK IT

FEEL IT

ACHIEVE IT

By the time I was 49, I had reached my goal of 50 rentals and I was living the life of my dreams.

When you reach a certain goal, your view changes. Do the process again: find your next burning desire, commit to your next goal, and let your decision guide your choices in every way.

The mind can only achieve what the mind can see.

Most successful people make decisions quickly and change their minds slowly once a decision has been reached. People who make decisions quickly and firmly, who have a burning desire and definiteness of purpose, generally get what they want.

Once you have decided to move forward, in your real estate career or in any endeavor that matters to you, it is imperative to get into action immediately. Start to learn everything you can about your geographical area, the market, and the area of real estate you want to pursue. If you find a mentor who has what you want, make an alliance, and learn from someone who has been there and done that. Genuinely successful people are often happy to share what they know.

You'll want to find the reason why you want to be in real estate and understand what it will do for you. (I am using real estate as an example because it is what I know, but the method of a burning desire plus committed decision plus purposeful action works for any goal.)

The bigger your why, the more you will stay committed to following your dreams. It's your why that drives your desire, so there is no such thing as understanding it too thoroughly.

"What the mind can conceive and believe, and the heart desires, you can achieve."

- Norman Vincent Peale

Chapter 3

THOUGHTS

"Creativity is intelligence
having fun."

- Albert Einstein

"Change your thoughts and you
change your world."

- Norman Vincent Peale

We have all heard the time-honored saying that thoughts are things. "As a man thinketh, so is he." This truth is the reason we need to train ourselves to think in a certain way. Our repeated thoughts shape our lives. Everything we see, do, or have, whether we find it pleasant or not, has been created by our thinking.

T-W-A-H-C-D

Thoughts-Words-Actions-Habits-Choices-Destiny

Our thoughts are the words we say to ourselves, and this self-talk is the most important conversation you'll ever have. You must direct your thinking in ways that support getting everything you want.

Sound easy? Changing a habit of mind is never easy. Once you fully understand this, you will find it an enormous challenge. Most of us are conditioned to negative and ineffective thinking. But you must persevere, because aligning your self-talk with a burning desire and committed decision is the most important thing you can do.

The words we tell ourselves will direct the actions that we take. Listen to your inner voice. Is it positive? Determined? Enthusiastic?

Are you replaying old mental "tapes" of self-doubt, fear or resentment? It takes time, but you can replace those with positive messages and goal-oriented thinking.

Thoughts lead to actions. Actions, repeated daily, become the habits that make us who we are.

Learn to direct your thinking and your actions will fall into place and become positive habits.

The habits we practice create our character and ultimately the destiny that awaits us. We are what we do.

The good news: The choice is yours! When we understand that it is our thinking that determines our direction in our life, we begin to understand the importance of disciplined, conscious thinking. You can direct your mind to direct your energy, and you will find that when your thoughts are aligned with a burning desire and decision, you're tapping into the energy and wisdom of the universe.

All day long, starting when you awaken, consciously cultivate the feelings and thoughts you want in your world. Your mind is your private place of power; what you think about creates your reality. If negative thoughts arise, don't beat yourself up. Observe them with detachment. They're just the echo of old habits. Let them fade, refocus, and carry on visualizing and strategizing toward your goal.

Cultivate a thought process that will move you in the direction of what you want to achieve.

Once you begin taking charge of your life by directing your thoughts, you will want be sure your priorities are in order. What is important to you? The clearer your priorities, the greater your ability to direct all your thoughts to building the life of your dreams.

Remember, this is your life, it is important. You matter! Make your burning desire, your decision, and your goals a priority. The people who truly love you will be cheering you on.

The Importance of Gratitude

You're rewiring your mind, creating new neural pathways. One of the best starting points is gratitude. Just about all of us have moments of gratitude in any given day, but to focus your thoughts on gratitude on a daily basis takes some practice.

Start each day by listing the things you're grateful for. Take a little time to visualize and cherish each one in detail. Make space for a simple gratitude practice as part of your morning routine, even if it means getting up a few minutes early.

The wonderful thing about a gratitude practice is that you'll see immediate effects on your mood, and that's a powerful motivator and energizer.

With a grateful heart, set your intention for the day. Say it aloud to yourself. Write it down. (A gratitude and intention journal can be a wonderful aid.) "Today I will _____ because _____." Taste your burning desire to make it happen.

Getting my mind in a good place and focusing on what I want to accomplish for the day has always worked for me. Remember, we get to choose what we think, which will determine how we feel and what we do. Gratitude and clear intention feels good. Feeling good and having a good vibration field will draw still more good into your life.

Everything is energy. Physicists have proven this scientific fact. There is an energy web that runs through everything, and the higher the frequency we put out, the better our life will unfold. Make it your first job every day to get yourself vibrating at a high frequency.

Thoughts are things. That is why the way we think is so important. The things we read or watch, the people we associate with, all affect the energy we put into the world. Build your thoughts with care, nourish them with quality input from mentors and other worthwhile sources.

Your life experience is a direct expression of your inner thoughts.

Directing your thinking is the most important process in creating your life exactly as you want it.

"Your world is your kaleidoscope, you choose the colors you see"

- Marc Pelletz

Chapter 4

FAITH

"We never grow closer to God
when we just live life.

It takes deliberate,
pursuit and attentiveness."

- Francis Chan

There are two kinds of people in the world, those who think they can, and those who think they can't. They are both correct according to their faith.

Faith is something that can be created by experience, repetition and practice. Just like going to the gym on a regular basis or practicing anything you want to get good at, it takes time and commitment.

Faith activated sets energy in motion to allow everything in your heart's desires to manifest.

There is no better feeling than the heartfelt faith that God, source, spirit, energy or whatever you wish to call it is working and conspiring with you to create the life of your dreams.

Looking back at the last 20-plus years of my life, I've made it a habit of connecting with my higher power. I call It God. It doesn't matter what you call It or what your religious beliefs are; what is important is connecting with the Universal Creative Source. Artists, musicians and scientists rely on it all the time; it's here for real estate investors and everyone else too. The more time you spend connecting with the Source, the more you will trust It and your faith will grow.

You are co-creating your life experience with this intelligent energy. Adding your increasing, reality-based faith to your burning desire and committed decision makes anything and every-thing possible. You will find that you truly can achieve whatever you can conceive.

God, the Universal Source, is part of us and we are part of It, whether you're most comfort-able with a personal God, an understanding of quantum physics, or some other modality. Our desire, thoughts and commitment are the way we communicate with this all knowing being that is what we are made of.

We are made in the image and likeness of God, and when we truly believe this, we will know without a shadow of a doubt that all things are possible. There are many different pathways to connect with Universal Energy.

Over 20 years ago, I began a practice of writing to God (who I freely admit, I didn't know or understand) each morning when I woke up. Along with a gratitude practice, it became a part of my daily routine, and I soon saw the results. Thus began my certainty that there is a power that will guide and help me in all of life's journey.

The more time I spend communicating with God each day, the closer I get to the Source and the greater my faith is. Today, I understand "Ask and you shall receive," not as a pleasant saying, but as my objective reality. And the closer you get to the Source, the more peace, contentment and trust you will have.

Make this energy your friend and you will learn how to transform your desires into your reality.

I will ask you to keep an open mind and reach out. It doesn't matter what your past beliefs or upbringing are. There is a power available to us all, but it takes a desire to find it and build a relationship with it.

A morning ritual that gets your day started with gratitude and intentions expressed directly to this power will go a long way to create the life of your dreams.

In the morning we can create a reality-based positive mindset for ourselves beginning with a clear picture of what we are grateful for, what we desire and what we wish to become, imprinting new beliefs through habits that support our vision.

Everything exists for us as a possibility once we have built an unshakable faith.

We must understand the incredible power of repetition and habit. Don't be fooled into thinking there is any other way to change your subconscious.

All of the suggestions in this booklet need to be practiced and repeated daily to affect your neural pathways and bring about the reality of your dreams.

There is a thinking stuff from which all things are made that permeates and penetrates and fills the interspaces of the universe.

A thought in this substance will produce the image held in that thought.

Gratitude unifies your mind with that source, so your thoughts are received by that of which all is formed.

The vision of what is possible takes hold, and our realities and priorities change accordingly.

"Set your life on fire."

- Rumi

Chapter 5

GOALS

"Do what you can with what you have, where you are."

- Theodore Roosevelt

I am sure you have heard this before, but have you actually done it? Have you really written down your goals and shared them with someone else?

If you have never done this before, this act alone will be a starting point in taking the action towards anything you want in life.

If you don't have goals, you don't have a target to hit. How will you know that you have arrived?

Setting goals is one action that most won't undertake. It sounds too simple or too trite or too difficult. To be successful in life or real estate, you must be willing to do what most will not do.

Be a winner. Set your goals.

The more specific your goals are, the better this works.

The universe or energy web has a way of conspiring to give you all of your heart's desires, but It has to know what they are.

When I began goal setting when I was just over 20 years old. I began a practice of writing down my goals on index cards that I placed in my car, by my bed and on my desk. I wanted to continually imprint my mind with all of my specific desires.

This is a good time to get all your priorities in order, not just your business or real estate goals but all of them. The cleaner and clearer picture you have of what you want your life to look like, the better it will be.

Keep in mind that your goals can have some flexibility. You will only be able to envision what you can see from where you are right now. As your perspective evolves, so will your goals.

When goals are activated by a burning desire, underlined by a committed decision, and informed with daily gratitude practice and an unshakable faith, the thought will be fully impressed on intelligent source and will transmute into reality.

Make sure you have some short and long term goals. Make small goals that you can achieve daily, taking action steps in the direction of what you want. You'll start to see your progress.

When I began to acquire properties, I made a goal of looking at a minimum of five houses a day. This was an action I could take every day toward a larger goal: buying one house every week. I knew these actions were practical steps toward my desired destination.

BE AN ACTION TAKER!

To develop a **magically potent** mindset, begin these daily habits. Build your temple within.

Magically potent beliefs are imprinted into your subconscious according to what you believe is possible.

To build ourselves consciously, with purpose and vision based on the model of reality I'm describing here, is the ultimate creative act.

Start today by making goals and moving in the direction of everything you have ever desired.

Remember this is your life. If you want to accomplish more, be more and have more, begin now. Making goals will be your blueprint, guiding your actions and channeling your burning desire.

Activate the intelligence that wants all your desires to be fulfilled. I challenge you, pick up a pen and paper and do it right now. Don't wait. Something wonderful is beginning.

"Enthusiasm is one of the most powerful engines of success. When you do a thing, do it with your whole might. Put your whole soul into it, stamp it with your personality. Be active, be energetic, be enthusiastic and faithful and you will accomplish your object. Nothing great was ever achieved without enthusiasm."

- Ralph Waldo Emerson

Chapter 6

SPECIALIZED KNOWLEDGE

"Specialized knowledge
combined with right thoughts
will move you in the direction
of the images imprinted
in your mind."

- Marc Pelletz

There are all kinds of knowledge, but only knowledge applied in an organized manner will help you move in the direction of your goals.

In this book, we are talking about educating your mind to move in the direction of your desires. All true learning takes place through experience, so if you wish to be truly educated, don't just read these suggestions. Do them. Once educated that way, you will be able to take these principles and, with continued practice, be able to achieve anything your mind can envision.

In real estate there are so many areas of opportunity and so much to know that you will want to focus, build your expertise and specialize in a particular area. My area of expertise is flipping houses, rentals and rehabbing in a specific geographic area.

When I started my investing career, I read all the books and listened to all the tapes I could find on the philosophy I'm describing. I also trained myself to think like an expert, studying different ways to invest with creative financing. At the time I didn't have money, so creative financing was definitely called for.

Once I begin taking action on the desires I had, the universe began conspiring to give me everything I needed.

You don't have to be the expert on everything. Forming a mastermind group with others who have complementary skills will add to the energy field you're building, an energy field that will magnify and attract all that is needed.

Get involved in real estate clubs and networking organizations in the area you're working. It will help you to build your team.

When I began my career in real estate the second time, in Florida, I knew that I must understand value, so I began that habit of looking at 5 to 10 houses each day. Soon I had mastered the art and science of property evaluation and knew exactly how to size up a prospective investment, giving me the ability to act quickly and decisively.

All skills, in real estate and any other field, can be learned. When we have a burning desire and cultivate the discipline of great habits — gratitude, intention setting, faith, and clear clean priorities and goals — all things are possible.

In my real estate career I have rehabbed and sold over 1000 properties, and in the last 10 years I've done over $100 million in rehabbed flips. I did all of this without knowing anything about construction. Zip. I don't have to.

Early in my career, I began building my network at real estate investment meetings and clubs. The contractor I met 20 years ago via my network is still with me today. The universal energy field connected us.

Align your energy with the source by cultivating these habits. Take action toward what you want. The universe will continue to provide all that is needed. It works for me, it will work for you.

You do need to actually adopt the habits, take constructive actions, and rewire your neural pathways for abundance and success. You can't just read about it and think, "I should do that sometime;" handy as that might be, it doesn't work that way.

But you'll find yourself enjoying the process. It's a refreshing way to live.

Please be patient. Sometimes things manifest quickly and sometimes slowly, but they will always manifest if we have a burning desire, maintain our gratitude, set our intentions and carry out actions that bring us closer to our goals. Don't quit. Have fun.

What you become on this journey of mind training and motivational muscle building, in real estate or any other field, will determine the level of success you will achieve. The knowledge you gather in your specialized field is important, but secondary.

The primary skill that will move you toward your dream of financial freedom and independence will be establishing these habits of mind and action. Count your gratitude. Set your intention. Commune with your higher power about it all. Write down your goals and keep them always in your field of vision.

"Wherever you go, there you are." Take consistent, continued daily action. Build these habits. Train your mind to think in ways that energize you and support your success.

To achieve success in any area, our beliefs must serve us. As we sow we will reap; it's a universal law, and we must begin to think in a certain way to be on the right side of it. Once you have begun rewiring your habits and training your mind, you will find that it's becoming your nature. All things considered, it is a lot less difficult than continuing to sabotage yourself with negative assumptions.

Once we make a clear decision and implement these practices, we change the vibration of energy we are sending into the universal energy web. (Once again, everything is energy. We are energy. Money is energy. Communication is energy. Properties are energy.)

It's our daily duty to our true selves and each other: to raise our vibrations through our thoughts and actions, so that we will attract abundance and success in our lives. As we send out higher vibrations, the energy web sends back higher results.

As our beliefs continue to shape our reality, our newfound reality continues to refine our beliefs. Fresh sources of gratitude multiply. Intentions clarify. Creativity flourishes. It becomes our priority to imprint positive images and beliefs on a daily basis, to continue to rewire our neural pathways.

The knowledge contained in this book is but a beginning. Where you are today is the cumulative result of all your thoughts, habits and actions so far. What you attract, you become.

Your innermost thoughts and desires are what shape your character and destiny, and all of it is within your control with a properly trained mind.

Become all you can be. Good thoughts backed by continued right actions will always produce like results, just as bad thoughts can never produce good results. Like produces like. You cannot choose your starting point, but I promise you you can choose your next moves. By imprinting your thoughts on a burning desire, you can definitely shape your circumstances moving forward.

Remember, **successful people are willing to do what unsuccessful people are not.**

Technical knowledge in your area of real estate or life will be important to your success, but it will be secondary to your thinking process.

One thought, one decision, one day at a time, take baby steps in the direction of fulfilling your burning desire.

Make the first decision today. "I will become all that I can become by training my thought process."

To build our model of reality consciously, with purpose and vision, is the ultimate creative act.

Chapter 7

BUILDING YOUR TEAM

"Coming together is a
beginning. Keeping together
is progress.
Working together is success."

– Henry Ford

This chapter will examine team building in a real estate investing context. There are principals here that can apply to any independent business venture, whether it's real estate or catering or massage therapy.

Once you have decided to make real estate investing your career, it is important to build a team.

At first, you need to surround yourself with a small group of professionals. Include a good attorney who specializes in real estate and an accountant. It's important to set up your company and do things the right way from the start. Having the right structure and accounting practices will help you to avoid issues that could cost you money in the future.

As you begin to invest, you will want to build your team further. Whether it is people who will handle marketing, management, or construction, you will want to build relationships in a certain way.

Set a tone from the beginning. Consider these people your partners on the road to your dreams. Get to know them as people. Build you inner circle with trust, honesty, and communication. Seek to inspire. As the saying goes, they don't care how much you know till they know how much you care.

It may be tempting to find the least expensive people to do the jobs, but this is not always the best way. As they say, you usually get what you pay for.

Always do what you say you'll do. Pay when payment is due. Be a person of integrity in all situations. Nothing will take you further than always being responsible and doing the right thing. It's another way of keeping the vibrations on the highest level and recruiting the universe to your cause.

Find the right people and delegate. If you are going to build a rental portfolio, it's best to hire a property manager to handle your rentals sooner rather than later.

You may think doing your own property management will save money or give you tighter control. But a good property management company will save your time, money and aggravation. If you really want to have a life and financial freedom, it's wise to start doing things in a certain way from the start.

It took me a little time before I was able to let go of managing my own properties. But once I did, I was able to scale my business, take vacations, and actually make more money.

Each of us has different abilities. Make an honest self assessment and decide what your interests, strengths and weakness are, then begin to piece together the team to complement your abilities and fill in the gaps.

As your business continues to grow, you will want to surround yourself with key people that understand your long and short term goals. Getting your people involved, making them feel special, and letting them know you care goes a long way in building a team that will be beside you for the duration.

Share your mindset freely. Helping other people get what they desire goes a long way toward keeping a group together for a long time, and helps you to achieve your goals. Avoid "preaching," but demonstrate by your example the benefits of a burning desire, gratitude, focused intention, goal setting and action. Create a positive feedback loop: you, your team, and the universal creative force.

Keep in mind, you are in this for the duration. You have a burning desire to succeed in real estate and build the life of your dreams. So, take no shortcuts in choosing and nurturing the team. Decide what type of company you want to create and begin to assemble the team with clear, defined intention, and you'll create a future that you can be proud of.

We can accomplish more as a team than we can ever do by ourselves.

It is the journey that really matters. Build your team wisely, with intention, and you will have taken major strides in the direction of a future beyond your wildest dreams.

Chapter 8

GRATITUDE

"Cultivate the habit of gratitude
for every good thing that comes
to you and give thanks
continuously. And because
all things have contributed
to your advancement,
you should include all things
in your advancement."

– Ralph Waldo Emerson

Gratitude is the elixir that activates a closer connection to intelligent substance.

When we have a grateful attitude, all the little things in life that can get in the way of our joy and happiness disappear.

An attitude of gratitude needs to be cultivated and practiced. A daily routine is best.

Start and end each day by thinking of three things you are grateful for. Spend at least one minute on each of them. Implant the feelings of gratitude into your whole being. Doing this practice morning and night will speed and reinforce the process of changing your neural pathways.

Being in and thinking from a place of gratitude bring us into harmony with all that is available.

When we live life with a feeling of gratitude, our energy vibrates at a higher frequency. Make it a daily goal to vibrate at the highest frequency possible.

Remember, this does take practice. To create change, we must make it a habit to be grateful.

You have heard it before: attitude creates altitude. Life is defined not by what happens to us, which we cannot control, but by our attitude to and perception of what happens.

I used to think I had lots of problems. Usually, I would blame someone else for them. As I began to grow, and learn, problems became challenges, which was a better way to look at things. As I cultivate a grateful attitude, all of my challenges became opportunities to learn and grow.

Learning and growing is a good thing. Reframing problems as learning opportunities is a much more useful way to perceive things. When we believe like this, we are liberated. Everything that happens to us is good.

There's an ancient Latin saying: Amor fati. Love your fate. When you can embrace all that happens as it just is, with acceptance and a peaceful mind, the practice of gratitude has been finally imprinted on your own subconscious.

The grateful mind continues to expect good things to happen, and this creates more good in your life. A feeling of "everything I touch turns to gold" is an energy that actively creates reality, just like someone who constantly says "Nothing ever works out for me, I only have awful luck," is likely to keep experiencing exactly that reality.

This gets us back to our original premise. Thoughts are things, and when we accept this as the truth , we realize the importance of directing our own thinking.

Thought impressed on intelligent substance will transmute and become that which we think about.

Therefore, it is of utmost importance to start the practice of gratitude.

When we have implemented the practice of gratitude so consistently that it is our natural state, and we embrace challenge with exuberance, anything and everything that happens is transformed.

Minor nuisances of life will be learning opportunities instead of problems, and still more opportunities will appear on your horizons. Your body and mind will begin to function like a GPS. Anytime you take a wrong turn or think a thought that doesn't serve you, you'll find that you can automatically reset and get to gratitude.

When your thinking is directed by your consciousness in a way that serves you and is connected to intelligent source, your decision making operates at a high level. Make it a practice to raise your vibration by activating the power of gratitude daily.

Each of us has the responsibility to choose visions and attitudes that will empower us. It's free. It's something any human being can choose to do.

So choose today to start the practice of gratitude, and watch as your life unfolds in a magical way.

Chapter 9

STAND ALONE PROPERTIES

"When you buy stand alone properties, it is only matter of time before you experience financial freedom."

- Marc Pelletz

Each time I began in real estate, I didn't have money. I had to make sure that every property that I bought could "stand alone". What that means is that when I buy a property, it needs to rent for enough money to cover all the expenses: taxes, insurance, vacancies, repairs and management. When I began my career, I knew I wanted a portfolio of stand-alone rentals and would do whatever necessary to acquire them.

It was important that each property have positive cash flow. That is why I started with multi-family properties, which seem to work better as stand alones. My goal was to acquire as many as possible, collect rents, and pay down the mortgage balances. I practiced constant, consistent daily action toward that goal. If you intend to be in real estate for the long haul, this is the best way to build financial freedom.

Wherever you are in your real estate career, I think you will agree that $10,000 per month in positive cash flow makes a good first goal to strive for. Start with a plan. Train your mind. Be patient. Constant movement in the direction of what you want will give you rewards.

Do not get distracted by thinking this is the wrong time to buy. There are always opportunities in all real estate cycles. It is always time to buy if you can structure the deal to meet your needs and buy stand alone properties.

When I bought my first small apartment complex, I didn't know it at the time, but it turned out I'd bought at the highest point of the market. My asset sheet fluctuated in value, but the cash flow basically stayed the same. At one point, the value dropped to $500,000; at another it was

$1.5 million. But I bought this property for my future, and the cash flow from it never changed. Almost 20 years later, there is no balance on it.

That's what building a rental portfolio of stand alone properties and consistently paying down mortgages will do: lead you to freedom. If you'd like a life of freedom, real estate rental properties are the best way to go, especially when you have the right management to handle them. Whether your goal is 10 houses, 100 properties or 1000 rentals, you can begin your process now.

Chapter 10

GIVING BACK

"Only by giving you are able
to receive more than you
already have."

- Jim Rohn

The more we give, the more we get. I have found this to be true throughout my life.

As Zig Ziglar says, "You can get everything in life you want if you will just help enough other people get what they want."

One of the greatest gifts of being a successful real estate investor is having the financial freedom and time to be more, to have more and to do more.

We continue to grow as individuals as we move from survival mode to success to having ever greater ability to make a difference and contribute in the world.

We continue to grow, cultivating thoughts and practices that move us in the direction of all of our dreams and desires.

As we evolve into fully integrated individuals, we find that place in our hearts that desires to give back and make a difference growing stronger and clearer each day. Gratitude inspires us. A burning desire drives us.

Right now, today, no matter where you are, there is some small thing you can do that will make another person's day better. Something you can give. Find it. Do it. Be grateful for it. Do another one tomorrow.

Now imagine having the time and financial resources to find ways to make lots of things better for lots of people. Take it from me. It's a **lot** of fun.

"We make a living by what we do, but we make a life by what we give."

- Winston Churchill

Chapter 11

HABITS - PUTTING IT ALL TOGETHER

"Good habits are crafted in the workshop of everyday life."

- Marc Pelletz

We understand now that thoughts are things, and that we have the ability to direct our thinking to create the life of our dreams.

To do this and to actively change our neural pathways we know that we must implement new habits and keep practicing them diligently until the neural pathways are rewired and the reward cycle kicks in, by which time you will be hooked.

Our thoughts direct the words we say to ourselves and others. These words direct our actions and habits, which in turn create our character and destiny. The road to fulfillment, the road to success, and the high road are one and the same path.

It is our responsibility on a daily basis to implement disciplines which will move us in the direction of our desires. When we do that, we stop blaming other people or bad luck or anything else and develop the ability to manifest what we need.

As I sit here finishing this booklet that I have had a desire to write for more than 3 decades, it is apparent to me that I followed the formula outlined in this book to make it happen.

About 3 months ago, I made a decision: that when I came to Breckenridge for Christmas and New Years, I would write this book. I have had a desire to do it for years. I worked myself into a **burning desire,** set a deadline, and shared with several of my partners. We made a date for a seminar to coincide with the launch of this book, *Think Like a Real Estate Investor.* The **intention** was firmly established.

I set my **goal.** Each day I would complete one chapter.

Now watch what the universe did. What God's brought to the table.

Before I came here I met a guy, Eric, while I was doing a real estate deal. He connected me with his friend Pete, who lives here in Breckenridge. It turns out Pete has written several books. We connected, and with his help and resources, my plan to have this book completed has been expedited. I'm ahead of schedule, and the pieces just keep falling into place.

There you go. That's manifestation. You're reading it right now. That's what happens when we direct our thinking, fueled by a burning desire.

Daily persistent action in the direction of what I want has led to this book being written in less than two weeks.

This book is meant to be a starting point for your success in real estate investing. The mind training principles and habits are useful to anyone desiring to walk a prosperous and honorable path.

Each chapter gives you a nugget of insight into necessary steps, a template on which to build each day.

You will want to continue to learn all about the area of real estate you choose, while understanding that **it is your thoughts that create your reality.**

Spend time daily directing your thinking. Build an unwavering belief that you will create everything your heart desires.

Take this information and run with it. Implement a daily practice of directing your thoughts. Practice gratitude. You will build a life that you are consciously co-creating each day with the Universal Source as a partner on your team.

How far and fast you travel will be dependent on your commitment to excellence and your daily practice of directing your thinking, backed by faith.

SUMMARY

Hopefully, you have found some wisdom in this blend of mind training strategies and beginning real estate tips that will motivate and inspire you to start today.

Implement these techniques on a daily basis, and begin to watch as the magic unfolds and things fall into place as thoughts aline with the creative source. Thoughts are things, and it is our responsibility to shape our thoughts and direct our thinking in ways that move us in the direction of our heart's desires.

Each of these chapters is but a starting point. Every action described in this book will take a commitment to daily practice and consistent improvement.

In creating the life of our dreams, what we do for a living is not as important as what we become.

Real estate can be the vehicle that allows us to grow: to become more, to have more and to help others.

I hope you find this book helpful and that it leads you on your journey to joy, fulfillment and financial freedom.

SUGGESTED READINGS

1. Think and Grow Rich *Napoleon Hill*
2. The Science of Getting Rich *Wallace Wattles*
3. Philosophy of Successful Living *Jim Rohn*
4. The Magic of Thinking Big *David Swartz*
5. The Bible
6. There's a Spiritual Solution to Every Problem *Wayne Dyer*
7. The Success Principles *Jack Canfield*
8. Unlimited Power *Tony Robbins*
9. Quantum Warrior *John Kehoe*
10. Science of Mind *Ernest Holmes*
11. Awaken the Giant Within *Tony Robbins*
12. Power of Intention *Wayne Dyer*

ABOUT THE AUTHOR

Marc Pelletz has made millions of dollars in real estate and has helped others to do the same. He's been involved in real estate for close to four decades, has been through several real estate cycles and has learned how to be successful no matter what the market cycle.

Marc has been inspired and motivated by many real estate experts and masters of motivational philosophy over the years.

From the Author

Life has not always been a straight path, and I've learned as much from my failures as I have from my successes.

Before I was 25 years old, I had accumulated over 100 properties and helped others build their own portfolios.

At 30 years old, I thought I had it made financially and was retired for life.

By the time I was 40 I was broke. Not just financially, but mentally, physically, emotionally and spiritually.

What happened?

After my early success, I got off track. I changed the habits that got me there. It was more than a decade before I realized what had happened. It was my thinking which directed my actions, and I'd gotten out of the habit of directing my thinking.

Then, somehow, with Divine intervention, I got back in step. I began again to use the process I am sharing in this book.

I began by deciding that I would turn my life around. I got a burning desire to do more, to be more, and have more.

It is now 20 years later. I have grown a real estate company, accumulated over 200 rental properties, and flipped over 100 million dollars of real estate in the last 10 years.

For more than a decade now, I have consistently earned a 7 figure income while having more time for family, vacation and self improvement.

The basics of creating a life of your dreams are outlined in this booklet.

I hope you find it helpful and use it as a guide on your journey to becoming the best you.

For more information please contact
Marc Pelletz
15 Paradise Place #164
Sarasota, FL 34239

mspelletz@aol.com

Any and all feedback is appreciated.

If you made it this far send an email to
mspelletz@aol.com

for 25% off my next book or event.

Made in the USA
Columbia, SC
01 April 2019